History for Kids: Greek Mythology

www.dinobibi.com

CPSIA information can be obtained
at www.ICGtesting.com
Printed in the USA
FSOW01n0502010515
6846FS

ABOUT THE AUTHOR

Jeannie Moon has always been a romantic. When she's not spinning tales of her own, Jeannie works as a school librarian, thankful she has a job that allows her to immerse herself in books and call it work. Married to her high school sweetheart, Jeannie has three kids, three lovable dogs and a mischievous cat, and lives in her hometown on Long Island, NY. If she's more than ten miles away from salt water for any longer than a week, she gets twitchy.

Visit Jeannie's website at www.jeanniemoon.com

For the latest news from Tule Publishing, visit our website at TulePublishing.com and sign up for our newsletter!

TULE
PUBLISHING

You won't want to miss more by Jeannie Moon…

THIS CHRISTMAS

Single mother Sabrina Gervais has built a happy life with her daughter Charlotte in their eastern Long Island hometown of Holly Point. Having Charlie meant putting some of her own dreams on hold, but Sabrina is content to surround herself with family and friends, safe from the realities of the outside world. She had enough of that when the man she loved broke her heart.

Jake Killen's career in professional hockey has brought him many rewards on and off the ice, but returning to New York brings back a flood of memories. When he sees Sabrina again, he discovers that he didn't just away from her ten years ago, but also from their unborn child.

Struggling with anger, guilt, and chemistry that's off the chart, Sabrina and Jake wonder if they can find love again and, this Christmas, make all their wishes come true.

Available now!

changed. When it came down to it, her life transformed when she met David. That strange day when she was swept away from her sorrow... and he kept on doing it, he kept making things better.

"Thank you," she whispered.

He looked down at her and grinned. "For what?"

"Loving me and loving my daughter."

One of his knuckles grazed her cheek and he shook his head. "God, you're easy on me."

Kate looked up into his strong face, looked into eyes that gazed into hers with all the love she'd ever wanted. David had no idea he'd given her back everything she'd lost. Even with all that had happened that night, she managed to smile and feign insult. "I am many things, David Burke, but I am not easy."

He chuckled. "True enough. But don't think that's going to scare me off. I'm here for the duration."

"Of that," she said. "I have no doubt."

THE END

thought the ordeal with Richard would have upset her, she was remarkably calm. Maybe she'd finally purged all the anger.

"You don't have to wait on me, you know." He was still wearing his suit pants and dress shirt, but his tie was gone, the collar was open on the crisp white shirt, and the sleeves were rolled up. Kate was enjoying running her fingers over the muscles of his forearm.

"I know, but I don't mind. You take care of me."

They were quiet for a while as he ate. "What time are you leaving on Sunday?"

"In the afternoon. We should get to our first stop by dinner time." The testing break in Laura's schedule was giving them a great opportunity to visit schools. She hated leaving David, but as luck would have it, he had a game in Boston at the end of the week, and they were going to see him in enemy territory. "You're sure you don't mind me taking your Rover?"

"Nope. I'd rather you drive that in case you hit bad weather." He'd started playing with her hair. "What's the itinerary?"

"We'll hit Cornell on the way up, and then we'll see Harvard, Holy Cross, Boston College, and Boston University."

"You know which one I'm rooting for." David had already bought Laura two sweatshirts and gotten involved in a phone call with Laura and Kate's dad about all the benefits to going to B-C. It was a running joke in the house, and even though she didn't say anything, Kate was going to nudge Laura in the same direction.

They went silent watching the news, and Kate thought about the last year and how everything in her life had

"I'll tell Marie to leave, then."

"No, Dad." She didn't back down, and Kate had never been more proud. "I'm staying here. I'm going to go on dates. I'm going to visit colleges, and I'm not going to be intimidated by *you.*"

"What the hell?" Richard looked at Kate. "Is she drugged? What did you do to her?"

Kate shook her head, amazed he was still trying to cast off blame. "Maybe you should listen."

"My whole life I worshipped you," Laura said, near tears. "And I don't know why. You told me lies and you cheated on Mom. You destroyed our family."

"Laura, our marriage was complicated." Richard didn't know what to do about the young woman he was facing. He had no defense against the truth.

"Complicated? You hit my mother. You *hit* her. That's not complicated. That's abuse." Laura stepped aside. "I don't want to live with you, and if I have to be honest, I don't even know if I want to see you."

Her daughter's final steps were to Kate's side. Her ex-husband stood alone.

He looked at them. *Stared.* And then, without another word, Richard Nicholls turned and left.

❧

KATE BROUGHT DAVID a big glass of milk, a brownie, and the bottle of pain reliever. He was on the couch in the den, tired, sore, perfectly gorgeous, and all hers. She tucked her arm through his and snuggled against him while he broke pieces off the brownie. Laura had gone to bed, and while Kate like you and you want me to calm down?"

Kate reeled back at his words. "A whore?" she repeated. "Like me?"

"Yes, like you. You think if you sleep with Burke he'll marry you? Why? Why would he want *you*?"

His words were meant to wound, and the insecurity she'd buried since she and David got together pressed against her heart. But what made her angry was hearing him call their daughter a whore. He could think whatever he wanted about her, but not Laura—he was not going to heap all that shit on her.

"She went on a date. *One* date," Kate shot back. "He's a nice boy. And I don't think you're in any position to question my morals."

"You don't decide, Kate. I decide. *I do.* And when I get full custody, you'll finally learn that."

The ticking from the hallway clock seemed to echo through the house until it was wiped out by the back door opening and David's footsteps coming across the kitchen. His face was red, his eyes dark, and he was ready to cut loose on Richard, until Laura stepped toward her father.

"No, Daddy. *You're* the one who's going to learn. I don't want to live with you, and that's what I'm going to tell the judge."

"Laura, don't be ridiculous."

David made his way over and stood behind Kate, his hands settling on her shoulders. It was a nice, secure feeling, but as she watched Laura, Kate knew everything was going to work out fine.

"I'm not being *ridiculous*. I don't want to live with you and Marie."

Contents

Introduction

No mythology is better known than Greek mythology. The amazing stories about Zeus and the other gods and goddesses hanging out in Mount Olympus are exciting and imaginative. The colorful characters in Greek mythology are loved by many to this day. Even some of the stories people write today are inspired by Greek myths!

In this book, you'll learn so much about Greek mythology. You'll find out the names of the gods and goddesses and what they were known for, read stories about heroes fighting monsters, and learn about why mythology still matters. We'll also talk about famous poems from ancient Greece that give us more information about what the Greeks believed. There's a lot to learn, so get ready!

Chapter 1:
Who Were the Greeks?

The Greeks were amazing people. Many of their ideas and inventions had an impact on every other civilization, including our own. Greece is sometimes called the "Cradle of Western Civilization" because of how much it influenced the rest of Europe and eventually America. "Western civilization" means the European way of thinking or a way of looking at the world, while "Eastern civilization" is the Asian way of thinking about the world. The Greeks certainly did a lot of thinking, and all that thinking led to some incredible accomplishments.

Where Did They Live?

As you might have guessed, the Greeks lived in Greece as well as some other small islands in the Mediterranean Sea. Greece has been around for so long, its history is divided into different time periods. First, there was Neolithic Greece, which lasted from 7000 BCE to 3100 BCE. Next came Helladic Greece from 3100 BCE to around 1100 BCE. The period that most people know about lasted from 1100 BCE to 146 BCE and is called Ancient Greece.

Map of Greece

What Was Life Like?

Life in any ancient civilization wasn't a walk in the park. Most people were farmers, and working out in a field all day was very difficult. Men could be politicians, actors, or in the military. Women mostly took care of things around their homes. If a family had more money, they might have a few slaves who would take care of chores.

What Did the Greeks Do?

The Greeks are best known for the amazing work they did in democracy, mathematics, philosophy, astronomy, drama, and literature. They also built amazing structures that are still standing to this day! Maybe someday you can visit one of these buildings, like The Parthenon or the Temple of Olympian Zeus.

Parthenon

Democracy

A democracy is a way of organizing the government. The United States is a democracy, for example. The very first civilization to practice democracy was the Greek city, Athens. They came up with a system that they called "demokratia," which means "rule by the people." That's exactly what a democracy is! It means that the people get to choose who will take care of the country and make the decisions. Before there was democracy, most civilizations were ruled by a king who made most of the decisions without asking anybody else.

Mathematics

The Greeks did incredible things with math. The Egyptians came up with a lot of the mathematical concepts, but the Greeks used them to do things like measure the circumference of the Earth and create geometry. That's right, if you don't like geometry, you can blame the Greeks! The amazing thing is that they didn't have textbooks or calculators to help them with their math problems. They thought of a problem, then tried to work it out using logic. Logic means to work out the truth using what you know about how the world works.

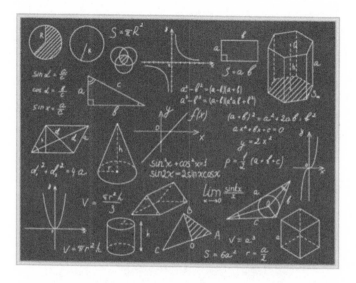

Green Blackboard Mathematical with Thin Line Shapes and Inscriptions

Philosophy

Philosophy is a way of thinking about our lives and puzzling out what it all means and if there are any rules. It tries to get to the root of every question, like "Why are we here?" and "What are we supposed to do with our lives?" There is no right or wrong answer in philosophy. Philosophers (people who study philosophy) try to think of what the best answer is then come up with guidelines for how people should act or what they should do.

Most well-known philosophers were ancient Greeks. They wondered about the world a lot and tried really hard to think of good answers. Some of the most famous philosophers from Ancient Greece were Socrates, Aristotle, and Plato.

Socrates

Astronomy

For a long time, people didn't know anything about what the universe was like. They knew how things worked on Earth, but when they looked up at the sun, the moon, and the stars, they had no idea what any of it was or how it got there. Most civilizations made up stories (myths) to explain everything they saw, and the Greeks did, too. They didn't just decide the gods had made the world and let it go, though. They wanted to know more. So, they tried to figure it out, and they did a good job.

Most people thought the Earth was at the center of the universe and didn't move, but a Greek named Aristarchus first said that maybe the sun that was at the center and the Earth was moving around it. If you didn't know any better, you might think that the Earth didn't move, so it was amazing that someone a long time ago guessed right!

Ancient Greeks observing the stars

Drama

Greeks were a dramatic bunch! Some of the main forms of entertainment in Ancient Greece were plays and theatre productions. As far as we know, the Greeks were the first to write plays and perform them in front of other people.

Literature

The Greeks didn't invent writing or literature (you can thank the Sumerians for that), but they did write some amazing works that you will probably read in school someday. We will talk about one of the most famous Greek writers, Homer, in Chapter 5.

When Did Greek Mythology Start?

Greek mythology has been around for a long time. But when exactly did it start? Who was the first to write down tales of Zeus and the other gods? Greek mythology probably wasn't written down for a long time, which means it was an oral tradition. Oral traditions are ideas and beliefs that cultures pass down through generations by word of mouth. One generation remembers the stories they were told when they were kids, then they tell their kids, and their kids tell their kids! It goes on like that forever until someone decides to write the stories down instead of remembering them.

The oldest written Greek mythology story that we know about is the Greek creation myth, which you will learn about in the next chapter. A Greek poet, Hesiod, wrote the story in 700 BCE. He called his poem *Theogony*, which means "generations of the gods." Now, it's time to learn exactly what Hesiod said about the creation of the universe and the first gods!

Hesiod

Chapter 2:
The Greek Creation Myth

We know almost nothing about Hesiod or what his life was like. All we know is that he wrote the first story we have about the Greek gods and how they made the world, according to the Greeks. Someone in his family probably told him the story, just like every generation before Hesiod had done, and he decided to write it down. Thanks to his decision, we get to learn about the Greek creation myth!

A creation myth is a culture's way of explaining why the world exists and how it formed. Creation myths usually involve gods who make the world, decide where everything should go, and who should take care of what. Hesiod's poem, *Theogony*, goes even further by explaining how most of the gods are related. Genealogy, the study of families and how people are related, can get pretty complicated, so don't worry too much if you get confused about the Greek gods' family tree. In the Greek creation myth, the world didn't start with gods who created the universe. It started with Chaos.

Chaos

Chaos was the first thing to exist in the universe. It was a dark void of nothing, kind of like an empty hole that goes down really, really far. After a long time, the first gods came up out of Chaos. These gods were:

- Gaia – the Earth
- Nyx – the Night
- Erebus – the Underworld god
- Tartarus – the other Underworld god
- Eros – the god of Love

Before the gods came out of Chaos, the universe had been perfectly balanced. Once the first five gods existed, though, the universe was unstable; it was in danger of falling apart. To keep the universe safe, Nyx (Night) created Hemera, who was Day. Erebus made Aether, who became the Atmosphere around the Earth. Gaia made the Ocean god, Pontus, along with Uranus, the god of the Heavens, and finally Ourea, who wasn't one god, but nine deities (gods and goddesses) who became the Mountains.

Gaia and Uranus fell in love (probably thanks to Eros) and had 18 children. Three of their kids were creatures called Hecatoncheires, who are wild looking, because they have fifty heads and one hundred hands! Gaia and Uranus also had three cyclops children. A cyclops is a giant with one eye. Uranus was a little bit freaked out by the Hecatoncheires and the cyclops, so he sent them to Tartarus (the Underworld).

Cyclops

The last 12 children of Gaia and Uranus were also giants, but they had the usual number of heads, arms, and eyes. These 12 giants were called Titans.

The Titans

The Titans helped balance the universe even more. Each Titan was the personification of an idea or something else that isn't usually in human form. Six of them were gods, and six were goddesses. The six gods were:

- Cronus – god of Time and leader of the Titans
- Coeus – god of Intelligence
- Crius – the Constellations
- Hyperion – god of Light
- Iapetus – god of Mortality
- Oceanus – god of Salt Water

The six goddesses were:

- Mnemosyne – goddess of Memory
- Phoebe – goddess of Prophecy (telling the future)
- Rhea – goddess of Motherhood
- Tethys – goddess of Fresh Water

- Theia – goddess of Sight and the Brightness of the Sky
- Themis – goddess of Law and Order

The Titans were super powerful and immortal. The six Titan gods all had several children who became known as the second generation Titans, except for the children of Cronus. Since Cronus was the leader of the Titans, his kids became the Olympian gods. You'll find out all about the Olympian Gods in the next chapter.

The second generation of Titans included Selene, who became the Moon, Helios, who was the Sun, and Eos, who was the Dawn (morning).

The Children of Nyx (Night)

Gaia and Uranus weren't the only gods who had kids. Nyx had a lot of children. Since Nyx was also Night, her kids were all gods and goddesses of darker and scarier things. There was Thanatos, who was Death; Moro, who was Doom; Oizys, who was Pain; and Apate, who was Deceit (lying). Nyx also had a few groups of identical children like the Oneiroi, who were the gods of dreams. She also gave birth to the three Fates who controlled the future and the lives of everyone, even the gods. The Fates were called the Moirai.

We'll talk more about the Moirai in the next chapter.

We could talk about all the children the first gods had, but that would take up the rest of the book. For everything that exists in the world, from Strength to Old Age, a Greek god or goddess represents it. Instead of going over all of them, we'll move on to what happened when Cronus became the ruler of the gods.

Cronus, a Terrible Ruler

Cronus

Cronus was not a very nice god. He heard a prophecy that said one of his sons would overthrow him, and that made him afraid. He really didn't want to stop being the leader. Instead of not having any kids, though, he decided that he would just swallow any children he did have. He swallowed five of his kids in total: Hades, Demeter, Hestia, Poseidon, and Hera. These children would eventually become the Olympian gods and goddesses. His wife, Rhea, had one more child, Zeus, but she was determined not to let Cronus swallow him. She gave Cronus a rock she said was the baby and left Zeus with Gaia, who protected and raised him.

Rhea presenting Cronus the stone wrapped in cloth

20

When Zeus grew up, he knew he had to overthrow his father because Cronus wasn't a good leader. He needed his siblings to help him, so he asked Gaia for help getting them back from Cronus. Gaia figured out a way to make Cronus sick, and he coughed up all five of Zeus's siblings. Being swallowed by their father made the children mad, so they were happy to help Zeus defeat him. Getting rid of Cronus wasn't easy, though. It took 10 years for the Olympian gods to defeat him. This 10 year war was called the Titanomachy. Most of the Titans fought against the Olympians. When the Olympians beat the Titans, they threw them all into Tartarus, the Underworld.

Titanomachy war of Greek gods versus giant titans

The Olympians made a new home for themselves that they called Mount Olympus. They decided who would rule which part of the world by drawing straws. Zeus won the sky and also became the king of gods and humans. Poseidon won the seas and oceans, and Hades received the Underworld.

Mount Olympus

The Olympian gods and goddesses had even more children to finish making the universe, and that's where *Theogony* ends.

The Creation of Humans

Theogony doesn't really talk about how humans were made, but other Greek myths do. One of

22

the Titans who helped Zeus during Titanomachy, Prometheus, took some mud and clay and made the shape of a human. The goddess Athena (whom you'll learn more about in the next chapter) breathed on the clay and gave humans life. Prometheus and another Titan, Epimetheus, were in charge of giving out gifts to all the creatures on Earth, including humans. They gave out things like claws, wings, and night vision. When they got to humans, though, they realized they didn't have any good gifts left to give out.

Prometheus felt bad for the humans because they couldn't do much, so he first gave them the ability to walk upright on two legs. This gift was a big deal, because until then only the gods and goddesses had been able to walk on two legs. He also gave them fire and taught them how to use it. All this would have been fine if Zeus hadn't found out.

Prometheus giving fire to humans

Zeus didn't like the humans. They looked too much like the gods, and Zeus thought the gods should be special. He also wasn't happy about Prometheus giving humans fire, because some stories say he stole the fire from Zeus or one of the other gods. Zeus punished Prometheus for giving humans fire by chaining him to a rock and sending an eagle to torment him for the rest of eternity.

Prometheus punishment eaten by an eagle

To punish humans, Zeus made the first woman, Pandora, and gave her gifts like sickness, death, war, and hard work. All these "gifts" were things that the gods were immune to, which made Zeus feel better. If the humans could get sick and die while the gods couldn't, then the gods were special. As you may have guessed, Zeus had a pretty big ego.

The bad gifts Zeus gave the humans did not bother them, though. They still built cities, got married, had kids, and did some pretty amazing things. A lot of the gods and goddesses you'll learn about in the next chapter even fell in love with some humans and had kids, who were known as demigods.

Now that you know how the world was made and how the first gods came to be, it's time to learn more about them.

Chapter 3:
Greek Gods and Goddesses

There are *a lot* of Greek gods and goddesses. There's Attis, the god of vegetation, Boreas, god of the north wind, Circe, goddess of magic, and so many more. Since there are just too many to name here, we're going to focus on the main 12 Olympians who lived, as you might have guessed, on Mount Olympus. That is, except for Hades and Poseidon, who preferred to stay in their homes away from Mount Olympus. Hades liked to stay away from the other gods in the Underworld, and Poseidon was happy in his home in the ocean. Let's talk about the Olympian gods first, including Poseidon, Hades, and a few others.

The Twelve Olympians

Gods

Zeus

Detail of Zeus in Piazza Navona fountain, Rome Italy

You already learned a little bit about Zeus in the Greek creation story, but there's so much more to tell! Since Zeus is the leader of the gods, there are a lot of stories to tell.

Zeus is the god of the sky, and he controls thunder and lightning. Whenever other gods or humans would make him mad, he would shoot lightning bolts at them. Zeus is known to have a bit of a temper.

Zeus

In ancient Greece, Zeus was everyone's favorite god. He was supposed to take care of humans, so people would ask him for favors or for help when they needed it. He was a god of justice, so if someone were treated unfairly, he or she believed

Zeus might step in and help. Since Zeus was so powerful, anybody who wanted to impress others would say they were related to Zeus.

While in a lot of mythologies, gods and goddesses weren't described very well, but the Greeks knew exactly what their deities looked like. Zeus is supposed to be tall and a little intimidating, with long curly hair. He laughs a lot and is very wise. In fact, one of the Olympian goddesses, Athena, was born from his mind and became the goddess of wisdom. You'll learn more about her later.

Zeus is also the father Hercules and Perseus, two heroes you'll learn about in the next chapter.

Poseidon

Poseidon

If Zeus is moody, Poseidon, his brother, is just downright bad tempered. He is the god of the sea and oceans. The ocean can be wild and unpredictable, and Poseidon was the embodiment of it. He is also the god of horses and storms.

Sailors would pray to Poseidon before setting sail and ask him to protect them. Before there was navigation and a way to talk to people on the mainland, going out to sea was very dangerous and scary. If you thought there was a man ruling the oceans who would keep you safe from storms and big waves, wouldn't you feel better?

Most pictures of Poseidon show him with a trident, which is a spear with three points on the end instead of one. He also rides around in a chariot pulled by two horses. His palace at the bottom of the ocean is made from coral and precious gems.

Poseidon

Poseidon and Athena liked to compete a lot. One of the most famous stories about their competitions happened when the Greek city of Athens was deciding on a name. Poseidon wanted the people of Athens to name the city after him, and Athena wanted it to be named after her. The two deities started a contest to see who could convince the people to name the city after them. Poseidon built a beautiful spring in the middle of the city, and Athena gave them an olive tree. As you can probably guess by the name of the city,

Athena won the contest. Athens is officially named after her.

Athens

Hades

Hades

Hades is the other brother of Zeus and Poseidon. He's seen as the outcast because he drew the short straw when the brothers were dividing up the world. He is the god of the Underworld, which means he also takes care of people who have died.

Hades rarely leaves the Underworld because the gods don't like him very much, and neither do humans. The gods don't like him because he's very serious and doesn't seem to know how to have fun, and humans are afraid of him since he rules over the dead. He does have a dog named Cerberus, though. Cerberus is a three-headed dog who guards the entrance to the Underworld. He's very friendly to anyone coming in, but he won't let people leave.

Cerberus

The most famous story about Hades is about how he got his bride, Persephone. This story is how the Greeks explained why there are different seasons. Persephone is the daughter of Demeter, who is known as Mother Nature and is also the goddess of the harvest. Persephone was beautiful, young, and very happy up on Earth helping her mother take care of plants and crops, which is why Hades decided he wanted her to be his wife. It's hard to get people to come to the Underworld, though, so Hades had to trick Persephone.

The Persephone's descent into the underworld

One day while Persephone was picking flowers, Hades created the most beautiful flowers in the world and put them near Persephone. When she tried to pick them, the ground opened up and Hades pulled her into the Underworld. There's a rule in the Underworld that you're not supposed to eat anything, otherwise you're stuck there forever. Hades knew this, so he got Persephone to eat a few pomegranate seeds.

When Demeter found out that her daughter was stuck in the Underworld, she became very sad. She stopped taking care of the Earth, which made it cold and miserable. Plants died and animals got sick. Zeus didn't want the Earth to be a lifeless place, so he went to Hades to see if they could make a deal. For six months out of the year, Persephone would stay in the Underworld with Hades. For the next six months, she could be on Earth with her mom and take care of it. This story is why there are two main seasons, summer and winter. During the summer, Persephone is on Earth with Demeter and the two of them are taking care of the plants and animals and keeping the world warm and happy. During the winter, Persephone is in the Underworld and Demeter is sad, so she ignores the plants and animals and everything gets cold again.

Ares

Ares

Ares is the god of war and Zeus's son. He represents the physical side of war (fighting). The other Greek gods respect him but are also a little worried because he can be very aggressive and pushy.

The Greeks didn't worship Ares much. Since he wasn't very popular, he isn't in a lot of stories. The ones that he is in, though, usually talk about him being embarrassed by one of the other gods.

Apollo

Apollo

Apollo is Zeus's son and the twin brother of the goddess Artemis. He is the god of the sun and light, as well as music and poetry.

In artwork, Apollo is shown as a young man usually holding a lyre. A lyre is a musical instrument that looks like a small harp. It was popular in ancient Greece, and anyone who was good at playing it was thought to have been given the gift of music by Apollo himself. All the other gods like Apollo because he is talented and entertaining.

The Nine Muses (goddesses who represent art, music, and poetry) are friends of Apollo and often hang out with him. The Muses are goddesses who inspire both humans and gods to make beautiful music and write wonderful poetry.

Apollo is also called the god of healing because he was the one who taught humans medicine and how to take care of sick and injured people.

Hermes

Hermes

Hermes is the messenger god and the god of sports and athletes. He is fast and runs between

Mount Olympus and the human world delivering messages back and forth. He is often shown in artwork wearing a hat and sandals with wings on them.

While Hermes is a nice god, he can also be a trickster. He likes playing pranks, sometimes to help people and sometimes because he just wants to. He is also the god of thieves, because on the day he was born he stole cattle from Apollo.

As the messenger god and protector of travelers, Hermes is also in charge of bringing the souls of the dead to Hades in the Underworld.

Dionysus

Dionysus, acient Greek god of wine

Dionysus is the god of the vine or the god of wine. Wine was a popular drink in ancient Greece because grapes were easy to grow in the area. He is also the god of parties and theatre because of his jolly personality.

While some of the gods were later additions to Greek mythology, Dionysus has been around since the beginning. There is evidence that he was worshipped in the time of the Mycenean Greeks, which is very far back in Greek history.

Dionysus was born in a weird way. His mother died when she was pregnant with him, and in order to save Dionysus' life, Zeus sewed him to his thigh. It might sound a little icky, but when you're a god like Zeus, you can do strange things. Dionysus was "born" from Zeus's thigh and became one of the 12 Olympian gods when he grew up. The other gods see him as an outsider, but he's a lot of fun so they accept him.

Goddesses

Hera

Hera

Hera is the Queen of the Gods. She is also the goddess of marriage and childbirth. Since she is married to Zeus, and in a lot of stories he often makes her mad, she is thought of as vengeful. Vengeful means wanting to hurt someone who has made you mad or offended you. Hera often punishes human husbands who offend their wives. Because of this, she is seen as the protector of women and children.

People worshipped Hera everywhere in Greece. In the past, childbirth was very dangerous, and a lot of mothers died while giving birth. Pregnant women and mothers would ask Hera for protection and to keep their children safe.

Demeter

Demeter

You learned a little bit about Demeter already when we talked about Hades. Demeter is the goddess of the harvest and is called Mother Nature because she takes care of the Earth. Her daughter, Persephone, lives in the Underworld with Hades for half of the year. Whenever Persephone is gone, Demeter cries and waits for her daughter to come back. Since she gets so sad, she can't take care of the Earth, so it gets cold and lifeless for half the year.

The Greek worshipped Demeter because she was the one who made life possible. She showed humans how to grow corn so they would have food, and she kept the Earth warm enough for people to live.

Aphrodite

Aphrodite

Aphrodite is the goddess of love and beauty. She is more beautiful than all the other goddesses combined. She was born in the ocean when droplets of blood from one of the Titans that you learned about in the creation story fell into the water.

Some of the gods were afraid there would be a war on Mount Olympus because Aphrodite was so beautiful. They didn't want to fight for her, so Zeus had her marry Hephaestus. Hephaestus was the ugliest god, so the others saw the marriage as a balance between beauty and ugliness.

Aphrodite is the mother of Eros, who is also known as Cupid. Today, we associate Cupid with Valentine's Day because he shoots arrows that make people fall in love.

Eros

The most famous story featuring Aphrodite is how the Trojan War started. You'll learn about the Trojan War in Chapter 5. In the story, a golden apple was only given to the fairest (prettiest) goddess. Aphrodite, Hera, and Athena all wanted it. They asked Zeus to decide which one of them should get it, but he didn't want to get on anyone's bad side. Instead, a human prince named Paris was told to choose between them. Each goddess promised him something in exchange for the apple. Aphrodite promised that she would help Paris marry Helene, who was the most beautiful woman on Earth. This sounded like a great deal to Paris, so he gave the apple to Aphrodite. The problem was, she had to steal Helene, which led to the Trojan War.

Sold his soul for gold

Athena

Athena

Athena is the goddess of war and wisdom. You might not think these two things go together, but Athena represents strategy in war, which means being smart about how you attack and defend. It's not easy to be level-headed in war. Since she is calm and collected even in tough times, the other gods love and respect her.

Athena was born from Zeus's head. Really! Zeus is also very wise, and one day he had a crazy bad headache. The headache turned into Athena, and she jumped out of his forehead fully grown. She even had battle armor on! No wonder his head hurt so much. Since Athena was born in such a special way and is good at everything she does, she is Zeus's favorite child.

You already learned in the story about Poseidon and Athena that Athens is named after her. After the city honored her by choosing her name, she became the city's protector. The Parthenon was her temple.

Athena played a very important role in the story of Perseus and Medusa, which you will learn about later.

Artemis

Artemis

Artemis is the goddess of the hunt, the moon, and archery. She is the twin sister of Apollo and is Zeus's daughter. Artemis was one of the most beloved goddesses in ancient Greek because of her role in protecting and caring for people and animals that can't care for themselves. Whenever anyone would threaten her animals or try to hurt women, she would attack them.

Since Artemis protects young women, a group called the Handmaidens of Artemis, comprised of nymphs and young girls, follows her and hunts with her.

Other Important Deities

Along with the main 12 Olympian gods, there were other gods and goddesses who were very important in Greek mythology.

Pan

Pan

Pan is the god of nature and one of the more important minor gods. The word "panic" comes from his name because he is said to make humans run away in fear without meaning to. It might be because he's a little scary to look at. The top half of his body looks like a normal person, but the bottom half is a goat. He also has horns on his head.

Pan isn't a bad guy, though. Since he takes care of nature, he's a little more wild and not "civilized" like the other gods. The Greeks didn't build any temples to worship him because he wasn't a god who lived in cities. Instead, people would build altars and shrines for him in caves and other places out in nature.

Hephaestus

Hephaestus

You might remember that Hephaestus is Aphrodite's husband. He isn't good looking like the other gods, but he is very good at making

59

things. He is the god of fire and metalworking. He makes weapons for the gods, and they're always the best weapons in the world. He also invents machines, like robots. Remember the Greeks wrote about Hephaestus long before robots existed, so they were way ahead of their time.

Just like Athena, Hephaestus liked humans and was happy to help them out. He taught them how to build houses and furniture, along with weapons. Even though he helped humans, the Greeks thought he could be destructive sometimes. They believed the place where he made all of his tools was inside a volcano, and sometimes he would accidentally make the volcano erupt. Some of the things Hephaestus made were a shield for Athena and arrows for Cupid.

Tyche

Tyche

Tyche is the goddess of luck and fate. Whenever something good or bad happened to a Greek, they thought it was because of Tyche. Since Athens was such a wealthy and busy city, the people who lived there thought Tyche loved their city and gave it more luck than others.

The Nine Muses

Apollo and the Nine Muses

Every Greek story or poem started with what was known as an "invocation to the Muses." The writer was asking the Muses to help them write an amazing story, and they were also thanking the Muses for the gifts they had been given. The Greeks thought that anyone who was good at something like singing or drawing had been given the talent by the gods and the Muses.

The Muses are all Zeus's daughters, and they each represent a different kind of art form. Their names and art forms are:

- Calliope – Epic Poetry
- Clio – History
- Erato – Lyric Poetry
- Euterpe – Music
- Melpomene – Tragedy
- Polyhymnia – Sacred Poetry
- Terpsichore – Dance and Chorus
- Thalia – Comedy and Idyllic Poetry
- Urania – Astronomy

When the Muses found someone worthy of their knowledge and gifts, they would give them information about one of the arts that would help that person create something amazing.

The Fates

The Moirai

Also called the Moirai, the Fates are three goddesses who control everyone's future. They weave threads together into one big tapestry, and every thread is one person's life. They are all the daughters of Nyx.

The three Fates were named Clotho, which means "The Spinner," Lachesis, meaning "the Alotter," and Atropos, "The Inflexible." They all had different jobs to do while they weaved. Clotho was the one who got to spin the life thread, Lachesis decided how long the thread (or the person's life) would be, and Atropos chose when to cut the thread and end the life.

The Fates aren't strong and powerful like the other gods and goddesses, but they control the lives of all humans, and even the gods can't change what the Fates decide to do. Only one god was ever able to change their minds about cutting a thread and that was because he tricked them.

Apollo, the one who tricked the Fates, found out that one of his friends was going to die soon. He tricked the Fates into letting him find another person to replace his friend in death. He couldn't find anyone, but his friend's wife offered to trade her life for her husband's. The Fates accepted, and Apollo became the only god who had ever or would ever change fate.

Chapter 4:
Greek Myths, Monsters, and Heroes

The 12 Olympian gods and goddesses you just learned about, along with many others we didn't name, play big roles in a lot of Greek myths. We will talk about some of these myths in this chapter. You will also learn about some of the most famous Greek heroes, including Hercules and Perseus.

Before we get to them, though, let's talk about how the Greeks divided up different time periods in mythology.

The Ages of the World

Geologists (people who study the Earth) and historians (people who study history) usually divide the past into time periods based on when a certain king or queen was in power or by which animals were on Earth. For example, historians call the time when Queen Victoria was the ruler of the United Kingdom the Victorian Era. Geologists call the time when dinosaurs roamed the planet the Mesozoic Era.

Greeks looked at time a little differently. Since they believed the world started when the Titans came out of Chaos, they kept track of the different time periods that came after that event. The myth of the Ages of the World, sometimes called the Ages of Man, tells about every time period since humans were first created.

Hesiod, the same poet who wrote the creation myth *Theogony*, also wrote about the Ages of Man. He said that there were five ages:

- The Golden Age – When Cronus ruled the Titans and the world was peaceful.
- The Silver Age – When Zeus became the ruler of the gods. Life for humans was a little bit harder than in the Golden Age, but they still had good lives.
- The Bronze Age – Humans started making weapons and fighting against each other in wars.
- The Heroic Age – Heroes and demi-gods were born, and for a while, life was the same as it had been in the Silver Age.
- The Iron Age – Humans started fighting again, and the world turned into a place of sadness and war.

In every age, something big happened that changed the future. Hesiod was a little pessimistic, because he believed that in every age, humans were making their lives worse. He believed he lived in the Iron Age, which was the age when humans would destroy themselves and the gods would abandon the Earth and humans. Obviously that didn't happen because we're still here, but this way of thinking tells you a lot about what life must have been like for Hesiod and the other Greeks.

Metamorphosis

Metamorphosis is when something changes from one form to another. For example, in Greek mythology, gods and humans would transform into animals. Sometimes the gods would turn humans into animals or other things to punish them, and sometimes the gods would turn themselves into animals in order to trick humans. Metamorphosis happens a lot in many Greek myths. We'll talk about some of them in this section.

Arachne

Arachne

Are you afraid of spiders? A lot of people are. This story is about how spiders came to be.

Arachne was a human who was very good at weaving. She thought she was an even better weaver than the gods. Humans weren't supposed to be better at anything than the gods, so saying this got her into trouble. Athena, the goddess, was very good at weaving and challenged Arachne to a weaving contest. Remember, a god or goddess gave any skill a human had. Arachne didn't show Athena the proper respect she deserved, which is why Athena challenged her. Athena wanted Arachne to learn that she needed to respect the gods and goddesses.

There are a few different versions to the last part of the myth. Different writers wrote that different things happened, but the end result is the same in all stories. In one story, Arachne won and Athena turned her into a spider as punishment. In another, Athena won and Arachne wasn't allowed to weave anymore, which made Arachne depressed, so Athena turned her into a spider so she could weave webs for the rest of her life. In every version, in the end, Arachne becomes a spider.

Zeus

Zeus transformed into an animal *a lot*. Most of the time, it was to make a woman fall in love with him. He even had to transform into a bird to convince his wife to marry him!

For a long time, Hera refused to marry Zeus. He knew that she had a soft spot for animals, so he transformed into a cuckoo that looked sick and helpless. Hera felt bad for the bird in disguise, so she took care of it. When Zeus transformed back into himself, Hera finally gave in and agreed to marry him.

Daphne

Daphne and Apollo

Daphne was a beautiful nymph. The god Apollo saw her one day and immediately fell in love with her. He tried to get Daphne to marry him, but she didn't want to. Gods usually don't like being rejected, so to make sure he wouldn't come after her, Daphne asked Gaia to turn her into a tree. Gaia was happy to, and Daphne became a laurel tree. Apollo took care of the laurel tree that had been Daphne, and to this day, laurel trees are the sacred trees of Apollo.

Hero Myths

In Greek mythology, heroes were usually demi-gods, which means they had one parent who was a god or goddess and one parent who was a human. They weren't as powerful as the gods, but they were stronger than humans. Since they lived in between two worlds, in a way, they usually went off on adventures where they would defeat monsters and help out the gods. Some of the most famous heroes in Greek myths were Perseus, Hercules, and Theseus.

Perseus

Perseus was a son of Zeus. His mother was a human woman named Danae. Perseus and his mother secretly lived on an island called Seriphos. They had to stay hidden because if Hera found out about Perseus, she would probably try to kill him. Danae's dad was also a mean guy, so if he knew about them, he might try to hurt them, too. Eventually, the king of Seriphos found out about them. Polydectes was usually a nice king, but when he fell in love with Danae and she rejected him, he was angry. Danae wouldn't marry him because she still wanted to be able to protect Perseus, so Polydectes realized he would have to get rid of Perseus before he could marry Danae.

Polydectes ordered everyone in his kingdom to bring him a horse as a gift, but Perseus and Danae didn't have any money and couldn't afford a horse. Perseus said he would bring Polydectes anything he wanted, so Polydectes asked for the head of Medusa.

Medusa was one of the scariest monsters in Greek mythology. She was a Gorgon, which is a woman with snakes for hair and a face that would turn people to stone with one glance. Polydectes didn't think anyone would be able to kill Medusa, so he was sure that he had gotten rid of Perseus.

For some reason, Athena and Hermes decided to help Perseus. They might have taken pity on him, or they may have thought that it was a good idea to get rid of Medusa. Either way, they told Perseus how to find the Gorgon Lair. He also got a magic bag to put Medusa's head in (since it would always be able to turn people to stone), winged sandals like the ones Hermes wears, a shield from Athena, a sickle from Hermes, and Hades' Cap of Invisibility.

When he got to the Gorgon Lair, he used the shield to see the reflection of Medusa. Only looking at her face directly would turn you to stone. A reflection didn't have the same power. Athena helped guide the sickle Perseus was holding and together they cut of Medusa's head.

In the end, Perseus was able to save his mother from Polydectes and gave Medusa's head to Athena.

Perseus with Medusa's head

Herakles (Hercules)

While Herakles is his Greek name, he is much more well known as Hercules. Like Perseus, he was one of Zeus's sons. Hercules was a demi-god who was extremely strong. Unfortunately, Hera knew about him and knew that he was Zeus's son. She tried to have him killed more than once, starting when he was just a baby when she sent snakes to poison him in his crib. Since he was so strong, though, he was able to strangle the snakes.

Hercules grew up far away from the gods. He learned to ride horses, fight, drive a chariot, and sing. He was bored, though, so he decided to set out and see if anyone in the world needed his help. He found out that a local army had been defeated by another army. He didn't feel like it was a fair fight, so he went to help the group who had lost. With Hercules as the leader, they won. This event made him a hero and even helped him find a wife.

Hera realized who he was, though, and wanted to end his happiness. By this time, Hercules had three sons. Hera made him go crazy and kill his own kids. When he realized what he had done, he was extremely upset and didn't know what to do. Theseus, his cousin and another hero you'll learn about next, told him that he needed to do something to make up for the crime he had committed. Hercules asked the Oracle, which is someone who is very wise and can offer advice. The Oracle told him he would need to complete twelve labors, or really hard tasks. The 12 Labors were:

- Kill a lion who couldn't be killed by any weapons.

- Kill the hydra, a monster with nine heads.

- Catch a deer with golden antlers called the Ceryneian Hind.

- Catch the Erymanthian Boar.

- Clean a huge stable that belonged to a king in one day.

- Scare away birds who were taking over the countryside.

- Take the Cretan Bull from King Minos.

- Take the Mares of Diomedes who belonged to King Diomedes.

- Take the girdle belonging to Hippolyte, the Queen of the Amazons.

- Take the cattle that belonged to Geryon, king of Cadiz.

- Find the Golden Apples of Hesperides.

- Find and take Cerberus, Hades' dog.

Hercules was able to complete every task, even though some were almost impossible. He was able to live happily for a long time after that.

Hercules taming the bull

Theseus

Theseus was the son of Poseidon and the most popular hero in Athens. The most famous story of Theseus is about how he slayed the Minotaur.

The Minotaur was a terrifying monster owned by King Minos, the ruler of Athens. It had the head of a bull and the body of a human. King Minos kept it in a labyrinth, which is a really big maze. The king would send seven boys and seven girls into the labyrinth every nine years to feed the Minotaur. No one in Athens thought this was fair, but they didn't have the courage to stand up to King Minos. That is, until it was Theseus's turn to go into the maze.

Theseus was just a kid when he got to Crete, which is where the labyrinth was. King Minos' daughter, Ariadne, instantly fell in love with Theseus. She didn't want him to die, so she gave him a ball of thread that he could use to find his way out of the maze.

Since Theseus was the son of a god, he was strong and brave. He was able to kill the Minotaur and used the thread to find his way back out.

Theseus and the minotaur

The Golden Fleece

Jason, Medea, and the Golden Fleece

Both Theseus and Hercules feature in this famous Greek myth, but the main character is Jason. Unlike the heroes you've learned about so far, Jason wasn't a demi-god. His father was supposed to be a king, but Pelias, who was his father's half-brother, took the throne instead. He even locked Jason's father in a dungeon so he couldn't take the throne.

An Oracle told Pelias that since he took the throne when he wasn't supposed to, one of the rightful king's sons would get revenge. Pelias thought Jason was the son that the Oracle was talking about and ordered him to find the legendary Golden Fleece. Pelias thought that it would be impossible for Jason to find the fleece. It turns out, it wasn't.

The Golden Fleece was the skin of a ram Zeus owned. The fleece was kept in a temple in Colchis and a dragon guarded it. Jason knew he would need the best warriors in the world to help him out. Fifty warriors, including Hercules, became known as Jason's Argonauts.

When Jason and his Argonauts got to Colchis, they asked the king if he would give them the Golden Fleece. They told him the goddess Hera wanted them to have it, which was true. The king pretended he would give it to them but said they needed to complete one task first. He asked them to plough a field using bulls that shot flames from their nostrils and had legs made from metal. Then, after the field had been ploughed, they were supposed to plant teeth from the dragon that guarded the temple. The king didn't tell them that once they planted the teeth, an army would come up out of the ground and fight them.

The king of Colchis had a daughter named Medea. She knew about her father's plan, and she wanted to help Jason. She gave Jason an ointment that would stop the bulls from hurting him, and she also told him what would happen when he planted the teeth. She told him if he threw a stone at the army, all the warriors would start fighting each other.

With Medea's help, Jason was able to finish the task. The king agreed to let Jason have the Golden Fleece if he could get past the dragon. Medea came to the rescue again by lulling the dragon to sleep. She knew her father would be mad at her for helping, so she left with Jason and the Argonauts.

They all eventually got back to King Pelias, and Jason gave him the Golden Fleece.

Dragon guarding the Golden Fleece

Mythological Monsters

Heroes wouldn't exist in Greek mythology if there weren't monsters to fight! You have already learned about some, like the minotaur, but there were a lot more. Monsters were usually the children of some of the scarier or meaner Titans and gods. Most of the monsters in Greek mythology, though, were Typhon's kids. Typhon is known as the "Father of All Monsters." Pretty scary name, isn't it? The first three monsters in this section are all Typhon's children.

Sphinx

Sphinx

Sphinx was a riddle-maker who had the head of a human, a lion's body, eagle's wings, and a tail with a serpent on it. Whenever someone couldn't answer her riddle correctly, she would eat them. In one myth, a hero named Oedipus was able to answer her riddle, so she threw herself in the ocean.

You might recognize the sphinx from Egyptian stories, too. The most famous sphinx is the giant statue in Giza, made of limestone and is 240 feet long and 66 feet high. The Egyptians built it sometime between 2558 and 2532 BCE.

Lernaean Hydra

Hercules and the hydra

A hydra is like a giant water snake with many heads. In fact, if you tried to cut one head off, two more would grow back in its place. Hercules fought the Lernaean Hydra and defeated it.

Chimera

Letter C with Chimera

A chimera is a pretty crazy looking monster. It has the body and head of a lion, a tail that turns into a snake, and a goat's head coming out of its back. If that doesn't sound bad enough, it can also breathe fire.

After the Greeks came up with the idea of the Chimera, other cultures started using it, too. Today, we use the word "chimera" to describe something we imagine that's too scary or wild to be real.

Pegasus

Pegasus

A Pegasus is a snow-white horse with wings. When Perseus cut off Medusa's head, a drop of her blood turned into the first Pegasus. Pegasus is a very regal horse, so he decided to fly straight to Mount Olympus and ask to serve Zeus. Zeus was happy to have him, so Pegasus lives with the gods.

One Greek story talks about Pegasus fighting the Chimera, so while Pegasus isn't a god or demigod, he's not exactly a monster, either. He can do good when he wants to.

The Sirens

Odysseus and The Sirens

The Sirens might sound like a nice, happy bunch, but they are tricksters. Sirens are bird women who live on islands and rocks in the ocean. They sing beautiful songs that make sailors want to go to them. The sailors who jump overboard to go to the Sirens always die, but no one knows why. Some Greeks thought the Sirens would eat them, while others thought they might just drown. Either way, hearing a Siren's song meant death.

The Sirens are *The Odyssey*, a famous story. Odysseus and his men were sailing past the island where the Sirens lived. All his men put beeswax in their ears so they couldn't hear the Sirens, but Odysseus was curious and wanted to know what their song sounded like. He asked his men to tie him to the ship so he couldn't jump overboard. When he heard the Sirens' song, he begged his men to let him go, but they knew he would die if they did. The ship made it past the Sirens' island without anyone dying.

Another story featuring the Sirens is Jason and the Argonauts. Instead of using beeswax, Jason brought a musician with him and had the musician play as loudly as possible. Jason's plan almost worked, but one of his men had better hearing than the others. When he heard the Sirens' song, he jumped overboard. He would have died, but Aphrodite saved him.

Chapter 5:
Homeric Poems

The Homeric Poems are two poems written by the Greek poet Homer. These two stories are very famous, and you'll probably read them in school someday. The first is *The Iliad*, and the second is *The Odyssey*.

Homer

There is some debate about who wrote these two epic poems. Some people think Homer was actually one person who was probably a genius because he wrote such amazing things. Others think that there were several authors who all added things to both *The Iliad* and *The Odyssey*. Either way, both poems tell us a lot about Greek culture.

The Iliad

Homer reciting The Iliad

The Iliad is set during the Trojan War, which Homer said happened from 1194-1184 BCE. No one knows if the Trojan War happened, though. It was supposedly a 10 year war, when a bunch of groups of Greek warriors attacked the city of Troy. Archeologists haven't found the city, so we don't know if it ever existed.

The Iliad talks about battles that happened during the Trojan War, and predicts what will happen after the Trojan War ends. *The Iliad* is considered a fictional story because it involves a lot of the Greek gods and goddesses. They all take sides in the war and help with the fight. A lot of people look at *The Iliad* to learn about how the Greeks viewed their relationships to the gods. The Trojan War started because Hera, Athena, and Aphrodite wanted to know which one of them was the most beautiful. This led to a woman, Helene, being kidnapped and taken to Troy, and then the Greeks fought Troy to get Helene back. If the three goddesses hadn't involved a human in their troubles, the war never would have started.

Helene

The Greeks often wondered how much the gods influenced their lives. In *The Iliad*, everything one of the gods does affects the outcome of the Trojan War. Because of the way Homer tells the story, it's clear the Greeks believed the gods controlled everything, and everything that happened to humans was a result of something the gods did.

The Odyssey

The Odyssey is a sequel to *The Iliad*. It happens after the Trojan War, and the main character, Odysseus, is trying to get home after the end of the war. *The Odyssey* also tells the story of Odysseus's wife, Penelope, and his son, Telemachus. While Odysseus was away fighting in the war, several men tried to convince his wife to marry them. Everyone thought Odysseus was probably dead, especially when he didn't come home right after the end of the war.

What no one knew was that Odysseus was trying to get home, but he had made Poseidon and Zeus mad. As a result, he was left stranded on an island with a beautiful nymph named Calypso. Calypso tried to convince Odysseus to stay on the island, since she was lonely by herself. He missed home, though, and he wanted to leave.

Athena, who had been helping Telemachus protect his mother from the men who wanted to marry her, convinced Zeus to let Odysseus go. Eventually, Odysseus made it home.

Odysseus had a lot more adventures throughout *The Odyssey*. He battles a cyclops, outsmarts an enchantress, and survives the Sirens' song. If you want to know about everything Odysseus does in *The Odyssey*, be sure to read the book someday!

Odysseus battles the cyclops

Chapter 6:
Greek Mythology in Today's World

We still read stories like *The Odyssey*, talk about heroes like Hercules, and wonder about how the Greeks came up with gods like Zeus and the others. But why does any of it matter?

The Greeks have a big influence on our lives. Believe it or not, the crazy stories they came up with are important. First of all, the Greeks were smart. They knew a lot about the world and never stopped trying to figure out more. The stories Greeks wrote are just as good, if not better, than books we write today. They didn't just talk about the gods and the things the gods did. They showed how the Greeks felt about the world and what their beliefs were about what was right and what was wrong.

Did you know that the word "myth" is an ancient Greek word? It means "speech" or "narrative." The word doesn't mean fake or not true. To the Greeks, everything they wrote was based on facts. When you look at myths this way, they become not just stories about gods who aren't real, but history books that are there for us to puzzle out.

A lot of the stories involved smart people doing not-so-smart things. There are still, to this day, lessons we can learn from Greek myths. They can teach us how to be more patient, kind, and forgiving.

Greek Influence in Everyday Life

All around you are references to Greek mythology. The brand Nike, for example, is named after the Greek god of Victory. Midas, a company that services cars, is named after a king in Greek mythology who could turn anything he touched to gold. We even named a type of book after a Greek Titan! According to mythology, Atlas was a Titan who was ordered by Zeus to hold up the sky for eternity after the Titans lost the war with the Olympians. We call books with maps in them atlases in honor of the Titan.

Atlas

Greek mythology inspired a lot of the movies you might have seen. *Troy*, *Hercules*, *Clash of the Titans*, and so many others are examples. The monsters and strange creatures from mythology are also characters in movies and books today. So you see, no matter how long ago Greeks came up with stories about their gods, we still find them to be amazing.

Conclusion

Hopefully you now know why Greek mythology is still so important to us. Not only are the stories filled with heroes and adventures, they also have lessons that we can learn from. When you read about Zeus and Hera, try to remember that jealousy doesn't help anyone, but you should also respect the people you care about. When you learn about Hades, think about whether or not you know any outsiders that might just need a friend. If you're an outsider like Hades, remember that it's not your fault. If you sometimes get really angry like Poseidon, think about how much better you feel when you're calm and cool like Athena. You can learn a lot from the Greek gods and goddesses, sometimes just by doing the opposite of what they did.

Also remember there is so much more to Greek mythology than this book could cover. There are more gods and goddesses and tons of myths that you can learn about on your own. Never stop learning more about something that interests you!

More from us

Visit our book store at: www.dinobibi.com

History series

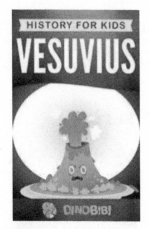

Travel series

Made in the USA
Coppell, TX
04 November 2022

85712323R00062